Christian Faith and Gender Identity

Christian Faith and Gender Identity

An OtherWise Reflection Guide

Mx Chris Paige

OtherWise Engaged Publishing

First edition November 2019
Cover by Chris Paige
Cover image courtesy of Canva.com

ISBN: 978-1-951124-06-9 (Paperback)
ISBN: 978-1-951124-08-3 (Kindle)
eISBN: 978-1-951124-07-6
Audio ISBN: 978-1-951124-09-0

Published by OtherWise Engaged Publishing
http://otherwiseengaged4u.wordpress.com

Visit http://www.otherwisechristian.com

Table of Contents

Abbreviations

NIV   New International Version

NRSV   New Revised Standard Version

Introduction

I often say that *OtherWise Christian: A Guidebook for Transgender Liberation* is the book that I wish I had had when I first started exploring my gender identity in my late twenties. However, I also wonder if I would have needed to start with a more gentle introduction—something written with less concern about scholarship and the big picture, something that would start by helping me reflect on my own experience. This booklet is an attempt to fill that gap.

The author is an a non-binary, transgender, OtherWise-identified person of European descent and Christian up-bringing in the United States, who has worked in and around transgender communities for more than 20 years. Nearly every perspective that I present here has been gleaned from others who have shared from their own generosity. I am writing *Christian Faith and Gender Identity* in the hopes that others will follow in our wake, sharing their own insights (with me and with one another).

The seven main chapters of *Christian Faith and Gender Identity* were originally written as a seven-day devotional series for *Our Bible App* and can still be found there. I am grateful for Crystal Cheatham's invitation to write. This edition is an expanded version, including an afterword, definitions, an appendix of related modern-day psalms, and ample space for you to make notes.

In that first launch, I got the most pushback about my interpretations of the Rebecca and Joseph stories, along with many opinions about eunuchs. Please understand that this is an intentionally short reflection guide. You can find more detailed arguments about scripture and scholarship in *OtherWise Christian: A Guidebook for Transgender Liberation*. This book is not intended to be a final word on any part of the Christian Bible. I simply ask that you open yourself to the possibility that there may be non-traditional interpretations that honor these sacred texts and shed light on transgender lived experience.

Each chapter includes a focus verse, as well as a very short summary of the related context from the Christian Bible. You are encouraged to read and review the full biblical text on your own. There is much more to be said about each text that I reference. In lieu of a formal bibliography, there are also a variety of short notes that are intended to help you identify additional resources to further your exploration of scripture.

Since language and best practices are constantly changing, you may meet people who will argue with the language that I use here in one way or another. Please use your best judgment as to what makes sense in your particular context and social location. The definitions are also terms that you can look up on the internet to gain more understanding through blogs and other resources.

Most importantly, each chapter ends with reflection questions. In the paperback version, I have left blank space for you to capture questions that come up for you, to make note of conversations you might want to have or next steps you might want to take. I have attempted to create a starting point, but the journey is yours to make as you see fit. There is space to write your own story.

That said, I am here and would love to hear from you about your questions and concerns. You can reach me at **otherwise.christian@gmail.com** and follow me at **otherwisechristian.com** or on social media.

With gratitude,

Mx Chris Paige
November 2019

Chapter 1

Who Are You?

God said to Moses, "I am who I am."
He said further, "Thus you shall say to the Israelites,
'I am has sent me to you.'"

Exodus 3:14 NRSV

Context: In Exodus 3, Moses has fled Egypt and is tending sheep when a burning bush catches his eye. He goes to investigate and learns about God's plan for him.

My first job out of college was with an organization that had a casual work environment. I typically wore jeans and a t-shirt to the office. Our office building was in a residential neighborhood and near an apartment that was rented to two adult brothers. One day on the way into my office, one of the brothers asked me, "Are you a boy or a girl?"

He was asking about my gender identity, and he was wonderfully transparent about why he needed to know. He wanted to speak respectfully to me. I do not know what language we used back then (though we might say "on the spectrum" today), but he was clearly very intentional and self-conscious about social graces—much more than most neurotypical people are. He knew that there was an appropriate way that you should talk to a lady that is different than how you might talk with a man.

I had short hair, did not wear make-up, and used a gender-neutral name. My chest was neither especially large nor especially flat. There were no tell-tale cues to help him make assumptions. He was not asking me about my sexual identity. He was not asking me who I was

1

attracted to (romantically or sexually). Gender identity has to do with who you are on the inside. It has to do with who you are deep down.

Like most of us, this gentleman had been taught that there are two and only two genders, so he was looking for a simple answer ("boy" or "girl"). The conventions around "boys and girls," "men and women," "male and female" over-simplify this question in a hundred different ways, but essentially he was asking, "Who are you?" and "How do you fit into my world?"

Not all cultures over-simplify like this. Classical Judaism had six genders. The words (Hebrew and Greek) for "eunuch" appear 50 times in the Christian Bible. In indigenous cultures around the world, there are many gender identities other than "male" and "female" such as *fa'afafine*, *waria*, *muxe*, and *hijra*. In contemporary Western culture, words like "transgender," "genderqueer," "gender non-conforming," and "non-binary" have started to give us more language to talk about diverse gender experiences. Words like these are important because they help us to talk about the diversity of God's good and gender-full creation.

I feel as if this tension around language may be similar to Moses' encounter with God in Exodus 3. Moses started out, tending his flock, minding his own business, and then became curious about this bush that was burning but not consumed. He went to investigate. Once God finally gets his attention, God blurts out a whole bunch of details, but none of those details apparently satisfies Moses. Finally, Moses asks God for a name. Moses wanted a short summary that he could tell the people back home: "Who are you?" and "How do you fit into my world?"

God responds with "I am who I am"—and these four Hebrew letters, YHWH, would go on to become the most sacred of names for God in the Jewish tradition. Yet, taking the name "I AM" also avoids the question in some ways. It is an answer that is a non-answer. "I AM" is a God who refuses to be boxed in with labels. "I AM" is a God who embraces change and lays claim to a story that is not yet fully revealed.

As a person with a non-binary gender experience (not "male" or "female"), I still need to use words to explain my gender, but I also love the freedom of knowing that I am made in the image of this defiant and open-ended God who is "I AM." This God gives me permission to be who I am, too—beyond the labels and categories that

2

might make some people more comfortable.

As you move through this series of devotionals, you will have the opportunity to reflect on how you, too, are made in the image of this defiant and open-ended God who is "I AM." How is your understanding of your truest self in process and yet unfolding? Do any of the labels or names that you have been given not seem to fit you perfectly? Is there a "real" *you* that is yet to be revealed to the world? What are the words you have yet to claim for yourself?

You are loved. When you are asking for clarification. When you are looking for the right words. When you resist labels. You are loved.

With gratitude to Dr. Audre Lorde for encouraging us to find the words that we need.

Related Terms

Sexual Identity or Sexual Orientation - Refers to emotional, romantic, or sexual attraction to a particular kind or kinds of people. Common examples include gay, lesbian, same-gender-loving, bisexual.

Gender Identity - Refers to someone's internal sense of their own gender (which may or may not align with the gender assigned at birth).

Non-Binary Gender - Refers to any of a variety of gender identities that are not exclusively masculine or feminine. Non-binary gender identities fall outside of the gender binary, whereas "man" and "woman" are a part of the gender binary.

YOUR NOTES

Chapter 2

Made in the Image of God

> *So God created humankind in his image,*
> *in the image of God he created them;*
> *male and female he created them.*

Genesis 1:27 NRSV

Context: Genesis 1 is the first story of creation (there is a second in Genesis 2). On the sixth day of creation, God makes humankind.

This verse from the first creation story is one that trans-antagonistic Christians like to throw around as "proof" that there are two and only two genders. Yet, scholars point out that "male and female" is actually a figure of speech, called a *merism*. It is not an all-inclusive list, but rather just two examples of many possibilities being presented in a poetic manner. Similarly, when the text says, "night" and "day," it neither eliminates nor ignores dawn and dusk. When the text says, "water under the sky" and "dry land," we don't argue that beaches, swamps, and marshes are against God's plan for the world.

Similarly, the rabbis of old would not have read Genesis 1:27 as suggesting that there are two and only two genders. Jewish tradition records in-depth conversations about how the text changes from singular to plural, as well as what the gender of the first human must have been. Good theologians like to remind us that all of our god-language is metaphorical—that we usually talk about God in terms that we can relate to even though God is something else altogether. Yet, these images remain powerful metaphors that shape how we relate to one another.

Since all humans (of all genders) are made in the image of God, we might actually argue that God is necessarily intersex. In other words, God must have both male and female aspects. We also see this in scripture where God is treated as male (he, king, lord, father) as well as female (she, a mother nursing or giving birth; a mother hen, eagle, or bear; a woman looking for a lost coin). In order for all of these metaphors to be accurate, God would need to be either intersex, transgender, or at least gender fluid!

Beyond all of this theological and metaphorical speculation, the important thing is that we are all made in the image of God, each and every one of us! Each of us holds some unique reflection of that divine spark within us. God is so awesome—so far beyond our imagining—that we need the diversity of God's creation to help us to comprehend how vast God is.

So which parts of God's image do you hold within you? The boy parts? The girl parts? Are there parts of you that seem to make others (or yourself!) uncomfortable? In what ways do you reflect God's intersex, transgender, or gender fluid nature? How does it feel to imagine that you are simply beyond comprehension, like the great "I AM"?

You are loved. With all your parts, each and every one. With your girl parts. With your boy parts. With your in-between and altogether different parts. You are loved.

With gratitude for the work of Rabbi Elliot Kukla and Rabbi Reuben Zellman shared through the *TransTexts* project (now hosted by Keshet).

Related Terms

Metaphor - A figure of speech that describes something in a way that is not literally true. It compares two things that are actually categorically different. For example, "Sarah is a shining star."

Intersex - A natural variation in the human form where someone is born with sexual or reproductive anatomy that does not fit the expectations for typical men or typical women. Some intersex variations are apparent at birth, but others may not be apparent until puberty or even later.

Gender Fluid - A gender identity that is not fixed, but varies over time.

YOUR NOTES

Chapter 3

Rebecca's Question

The children struggled together within her;
and she said, "If it is to be this way, why do I live?"
So she went to inquire of the Lord.

Genesis 25:22 NRSV

Context: In Genesis 25, we have an accounting of the lineage of Abraham, which moves us into the next generation. Rebecca is Isaac's wife and the mother of Jacob and Esau.

In Genesis, Rebecca and her mother-in-law Sarah were initially described as unable to have children. In their time and culture, women were expected to provide children for their husbands. In her book, *The Soul of the Stranger*, Joy Ladin describes the social dynamic around women's infertility as a "gender failure," meaning that these women had failed to fulfill the expectations and obligations placed upon them because they were women.

Ladin also talks about "gender surveillance," which is related to the expectation that we must somehow perform our gender "properly." In other words, when you are checking whether someone "looks" like they might be in the "wrong" bathroom, you are engaging in gender surveillance. When you, yourself, feel obligated to like or dislike a sport, wear or not wear certain clothing, or otherwise monitor your own appearance or activities, because of your gender, that, too, is gender surveillance. Gender expectations touch every part of our lives and create both internal and external pressures to judge ourselves and others based on cultural norms.

You do not have to be transgender to experience "gender surveillance" or "gender failure," but these are experiences that are particularly common among transgender people. For instance, I always knew that I was a failure as a "girl" and I couldn't even imagine being a "woman." I did what I could to try to play the part as I grew older and the pressure increased, but it just was not who I was. I was awkward and uncomfortable about any situation where my gender mattered.

When I was writing *OtherWise Christian*, Rebecca really surprised me. Rabbinic tradition had already raised a great many questions about Rebecca's being so strong, assertive, and adventurous, while her husband Isaac seemed to be submissive at every turn. Jay Michaelson goes so far as to call Isaac a "power bottom," though the tradition of Kabbalah (Jewish mysticism) simply says he had the "soul of a woman." I had all of these questions floating around in my head as I started writing about Rebecca.

In Genesis 25:22, after Rebecca has become pregnant, she asks a question, and the Hebrew for that question is unclear. In translation, it is rendered "Why is this happening to me?" (or "What will become of me?" or "Why do I live?" or "I don't want to be pregnant!"), but the actual Hebrew suggests that it is a question of "being" or "I AM"-ness (again evoking Exodus 3:14). The Hebrew is more like "This me?" which could be read as "Why am I like this?" or even "Why do I exist?" Somehow this pregnancy was making Rebecca question her very existence and/or identity: "Who am I?"

In context with the rest of the story, I finally had to ask myself about Rebecca's relationship with her pregnancy. We only assume that Rebecca wanted to have children because of what we have been taught about "women in that time and culture." However, other things about the story fall into place if we let go of that assumption: What if strong, assertive, adventurous Rebecca did not want children? What if it was *only* Isaac that was praying for Rebecca to get pregnant? What if Rebecca had done her best to avoid getting pregnant all those years and *that* was why she had been "infertile"?

While the physical experience of pregnancy "should" have been a time of celebration for a previously infertile woman, it bothered Rebecca so much that she questioned her existence! That struggle with her own body makes me wonder if her question is an indication of gender dysphoria. In other words, perhaps the physical sensation of pregnancy did not align with Rebecca's deepest sense of herself. Obviously, that is just one possible reading of the text. People often assume that she was just having a "difficult" pregnancy. Yet, it is clear that Rebecca struggled through her pregnancy in a way that had her questioning both herself and God.

Are there things about the way you experience your body that make you question yourself or God? Have you ever felt like you were failing at your gender? Has gender surveillance been more or less severe in your religious communities (compared to other areas of your life)? How do you cope with the pressures of gender surveillance?

You are loved. When you don't fit in. When you don't feel right. When you are struggling with expectations. You are loved.

With gratitude for Joy Ladin's *Soul of the Stranger: Reading the God and Torah from a Transgender Perspective*, as well as time spent together in Torah study.

Related Terms

Assigned Gender - An individual's gender as determined by others (such as doctors) at birth, typically with reference to one's genitalia.

Gender Surveillance - Scrutiny to determine whether one is male or female, made more consequential by fear of consequences for those who fail to meet binary gender expectations.

Gender Failure - Inability to fulfill one's expected gender role(s).

Gender Dysphoria - Involves a conflict between a person's assigned gender and their gender identity. People with gender dysphoria may be very uncomfortable with the gender they were assigned, with gendered characteristics of their body, or with the expected roles of their assigned gender.

YOUR NOTES

Chapter 4

Joseph's Robe

Now Israel loved Joseph
more than any other of his children,
because he was the son of his old age;
and he had made him a long robe with sleeves.

Genesis 37:3 NRSV

Context: Genesis 37–50 follows Joseph through various trials, starting with estrangement from and betrayal by his 11 brothers.

The harsh violence that Joseph's brothers show toward him is a bit surprising in Joseph's story. It is hard to comprehend siblings' selling one of their own into slavery—and nearly killing him on the spot—over a younger brother's petty petulance. It has also seemed odd how fixated the brothers regarding the "long robe with sleeves," more commonly called a "coat of many colors."

However, Peterson Toscano popularized a literal reading of the *ketonet passim* that makes more sense out of this story. Footnotes will often say "the Hebrew is unclear," but 2 Samuel 13:18b clearly defines a *ketonet passim* as "the kind of garment the virgin daughters of the king wore" (NIV). Toscano lovingly dubs it a "princess dress" and suddenly the story takes on new depth.

In a more extreme version of gender surveillance, Joseph's brothers were enforcing gender expectations and punishing Joseph for being an effeminate man. Reuben prevents them from killing Joseph outright, but the brothers take out their anger on the "princess dress" as a representation of Joseph's gender non-conforming identity, while removing Joseph himself from the picture entirely (or so they thought).

Anyone who has ever been called "sissy" or "queer" by playground bullies will probably recognize the dynamic. There is never *really* a good reason why bigger kids beat up on smaller or more effeminate kids, except to "teach him a lesson." What lesson? Usually, it is a lesson about gender expectations (and possibly gender failure).

As a female-assigned child, one of the things I learned quickly was that people do not always say what they mean. I was taught that I could "grow up to be whatever I wanted," but I also had to stand in line with the girls and was told (by a teacher) that "nobody likes a smart girl." Even growing up in a fairly liberal time and place, I got mixed messages about what was acceptable for me as a girl.

Have you been impacted by mixed messages and/or unstated expectations about gender? How have gender expectations been enforced in your world? What messages did you receive about gender as a child? Have those lessons served you well?

You are loved. When they try to get you to fall into line. When it hurts to be different. When you struggle to find your people. You are loved.

With gratitude for Peterson Toscano's *Transfigurations: Transgressing Gender in the Bible*, available on DVD and streaming via Amazon.

Related Terms

Gender Expectations - Particular behaviors and attributes that are generally considered acceptable, appropriate, or desirable for people with a particular gender (assigned or affirmed) in a particular cultural context.

Gender Non-conforming - Relating to behavior or gender expression which does not align with gender expectations. Anyone who goes against society's rules for how a "man" or a "woman" is "supposed to" act.

Affirmed Gender - An individual's internal sense of who they are, which may or may not match the gender they were assigned at birth. Affirmed gender is someone's actual gender identity, in contrast to their assigned gender.

YOUR NOTES

Chapter 5

Jesus and the Eunuchs

For there are eunuchs who have been so from birth,
and there are eunuchs who have been made eunuchs by others,
and there are eunuchs who have made themselves eunuchs
for the sake of the kingdom of heaven.
Let anyone accept this who can.

Matthew 19:12 NRSV

Context: In Matthew 19, this unexpected verse comes between teachings about divorce, children, and giving up wealth and family for the kingdom of God.

Eunuchs were an alternate gender in the ancient world, in a variety of cultures, and over many generations. Castration was the primary marker of a eunuch, but "eunuchs of the sun" were those who had ambiguous genitalia from birth (for instance, as a result of certain intersex variations). Eunuchs were part of a servant or slave class, though they were often placed in highly trusted positions within religious and political institutions. They were alternately assumed to be celibate or admonished for sexual impurity (that is, for reveling in freedom from fertility and its consequences).

Given this background, it is a miracle that such a provocative teaching from Jesus as Matthew 19:12 has survived to this day! Jesus made waves by hanging around with sex workers and tax collectors, by caring for the poor and the outcast, and by questioning religious and political authorities, but, here, Jesus is honoring this freaky underclass of eunuchs as a path toward serving God. Over several centuries, Christian authorities have tried to domesticate this teaching by reducing it to a conversation about "spiritual eunuchs" (for example, those who choose celibacy). Some translations replace the word "eunuch" with variations of "unmarried." However, there is no doubt that the early "church fathers" were actively arguing about Matthew 19:12 in the first centuries immediately after Jesus' death and resurrection. This has always been a controversial teaching.

So much of our interpretation of the Bible is shaped by cultural assumptions about what Jesus "must" have meant. Yet, Jesus clearly outlines three very specific kinds of eunuchs. "Eunuchs from birth" clearly align with "eunuchs of the sun" or certain intersex variations. Since castration was used as a means of punishment and subjugation, "eunuchs who have been made eunuchs by others" includes those who may have been forced to become eunuchs. The third category, those "who have made themselves eunuchs," means that Jesus was not just embracing people who had no choice in the matter, but also those who actively chose an alternate gender identity.

It is important to note that there is no sign of equivocation. Jesus does not "heal" the eunuchs. Jesus does not talk about their repentance. Jesus simply embraces the eunuch as a role model, while acknowledging that this is a teaching that will not go over easily with everyone! Some scholars have suggested that Jesus may have been called a eunuch as a slur, because he was not married as was expected of men in his time. Instead of denying it or distancing himself from the eunuchs, Jesus showed bold solidarity with them.

Much conversation has been had about who should be considered a modern-day eunuch. Arguments have included: gay men, lesbians, transgender women, intersex people, the unmarried, and the celibate. In my book, *OtherWise Christian*, I argue that none of these modern identities aligns perfectly with the eunuch because we live in a very different cultural moment. However, I also argue that all of these identities (eunuchs included) resist the rigid gender ideology that dominates our time—and so I group them together as "OtherWise-gendered" people.

Jesus taught in a variety of ways that submitting to gender expectations and cultural norms is not the plumb line for a faithful life. I have no doubt that Jesus embraces the wisdom and courage of OtherWise-gendered people (for example, transgender, non-binary, and intersex people) today, just as he did the eunuchs of his time. We, too, are role models for authentic living in a world that has worked hard to erase us. Thank God the principalities and powers of Christian tradition were not successful in permanently diluting the power of this sacred text.

So, are you able to accept this teaching? Will you accept this invitation from Jesus? Given his words about eunuchs, how do you think Jesus would approach intersex and transgender people today?

You are loved. When they want you to forget your ancestors in the faith. When they try to erase you. When you are claiming your place in the kingdom of God. You are loved.

Scholarship about eunuchs and Matthew 19:12 is explored in more detail in *OtherWise Christian: A Guidebook for Transgender Liberation* by Mx Chris Paige.

Related Terms

Eunuch - An alternate gender in the ancient world, which was considered to be somewhere between "male" and "female." Eunuchs were typically intersex or assigned male. If assigned male, they would become eunuchs when their testicles were removed or crushed.

Transgender - Someone whose (affirmed) gender identity does not match their assigned gender.

OtherWise-gendered - Someone with a gender identity or expression which resists the modern Western idea of two and only two, permanent and unchanging genders, defined easily by biology at birth.

YOUR NOTES

Chapter 6

An Ethiopian Eunuch Traveler

So he got up and went.
Now there was an Ethiopian eunuch,
a court official of the Candace,
queen of the Ethiopians,
in charge of her entire treasury.
He had come to Jerusalem to worship.

Acts 8:27 NRSV

Context: In Acts 8, the early church is trying to find its way in the midst of persecution. The Spirit sends Philip to an encounter with an Ethiopian eunuch who is baptized and then goes off to spread the Gospel to the ends of the earth.

The Ethiopian eunuch traveler in Acts 8 is a well-known story. This Black, OtherWise-gendered, foreigner instigates the first Christian baptism and then becomes the first Christian pastor and evangelist as he returns to Africa to spread the Good News of Jesus. Like Jesus, Philip does not "heal" the eunuch or admonish the traveler to repent of their history. The pair simply finds the first appropriate body of water in which the traveler can be baptized.

The traveler's question, "What can prevent me?" is loaded with cultural baggage. Philip and the early church needed to decide how they were going to proceed in building up the Christian community now that Jesus was no longer physically present. An Ethiopian eunuch would have been disallowed from worship in the Temple at Jerusalem.

So, Philip was faced with a choice—to conform to the religious conventions of Jerusalem or embrace this eager convert. In fact, some scholars argue that Philip's decision to embrace the traveler is just as historic for the early church as the traveler's conversion and baptism.

This story invites us to be transformed alongside Philip and the traveler. Who are the Ethiopian eunuch travelers of our time? Who seems to live so far off from the Kingdom of God that it is hard to imagine them being included? Who in our world might be looked down upon or outcast, yet invites or even demands that we make a commitment, like Philip? What is preventing us from rushing to their side as they travel on their way?

The story of the Ethiopian eunuch is so familiar to many of us that it can be easy to forget what these words mean. Philip was sharing the good news of Jesus with a Black surgically-altered, gender-variant person journeying through a wilderness place, far from the Temple. Philip offered assistance to an immigrant from a far-off land who was passing through a borderland. The traveler did not seek out Philip's assistance. God told Philip, through an angel, to seek out this wilderness place. Once Philip responded, traveling far outside of his comfort zone, it was only then that he had the opportunity to offer the traveler his assistance.

Certainly, all of these categories of folk remain at risk in our world today. Immigrants are being locked up in cages without access to hygiene or medical care. Transgender women of color too often die gruesome, violent deaths—and in the United States these deaths are usually Black transgender women. Leaders in political office portray all of these folk as predators and criminals. Yet, Acts 8 suggests that these are exactly the kind of people who were the first fruits of the resurrected Jesus. They would go on to found Christian churches in far-off lands. All of this happened because Philip was obedient and made a commitment to go out of his way to seek and find them.

Are you more like the Ethiopian eunuch traveler or more like Philip? Is God asking you to reach out into the wilderness places of our world to be in solidarity with people who are different from you? Or, is it time to embrace the unique gifts that you have been given to claim your place at God's banquet table? Indeed, what is preventing *you*? Acts 8 invites us to go when the Spirit calls us, even if it might seem uncomfortable or unfamiliar.

You are loved. When you have been prevented from joining in worship. When you have a choice to make. When you are hanging around with people who others might find unacceptable. You are loved.

With gratitude to the Rev. Eric Thomas for highlighting the importance of Philip as a role model for people who want to be allies to transgender people.

Related Terms

Gender Variant - A term that is used to generally describe people who depart from binary gender norms and expectations.

Gender Creative or **Gender Expansive** - Terms that are used to describe children and youth who don't "follow the rules" of their assigned gender. These terms maintain flexibility in terms of the young person's ultimate gender identity, allowing them time to explore and experiment without being pressured into a fixed gender identity.

Transgender Day of Remembrance - An annual observance on November 20 each year to remember those who have died because of anti-transgender violence. Since Transgender Day of Remembrance was established in 1999, the victims have been overwhelmingly young, transgender women of color.

YOUR NOTES

Chapter 7

Freedom in Christ

There is no longer Jew or Greek,
there is no longer slave or free,
there is no longer male and female;
for all of you are one in Christ Jesus.

Galatians 3:28 NRSV

Context: Galatians is one of the earliest letters—from Paul to the church in Galatia. Paul writes as Jewish and non-Jewish Christians are trying to work out their relationship with Jewish law in light of Jesus.

A plain reading of this Galatians text specifically suggests that the categories "male and female" have been abolished in favor of a new Christian unity. Indeed, scholars tell us that the early Christian communities demonstrated radical equality between men and women (and we might also speculate about eunuchs!), which was uncommon in their time. Meanwhile, the phrase "male and female" stands out as an echo of Genesis 1:27 pointing to how Christ Jesus is ushering in a "new creation."

Yet, we live in a world where gender distinctions still matter in small and large ways. We need to talk about gender so we can know how to treat one another with respect. The more we learn about gender, the more we will be able to see the fullness of God among us. Whatever our struggles with the realities of gender surveillance or gender violence, we are all made in the image of God. Thanks be to God!

Whether you are comfortable with the labels they have given you or whether you have struggled to make a way out of no way in the wilderness, you are a beloved of God. Jesus is in solidarity with us— not only in spite of, but perhaps even because of our gender failures and gender dysphoria. God has looked down and seen our suffering and sent us angels to bring us a good word. God has had compassion upon us and wants us to be whole.

Let us be encouraged—and like the Ethiopian eunuch traveler (and Philip), let us carry these blessings to others who share in our struggles. May our freedom in Christ provide us with a confidence that enables us to resist the many structures of supremacy that dominate this world. May our liberation draw us nearer to one another and to God. May God's OtherWise family continue to expand and to embrace all those who may be burdened by the boundaries and binaries of this world.

What does freedom look like for you? How might you need to be liberated from limited ideas about "male and female"? What part(s) of yourself do you need to embrace more fully in order to find the strength and confidence to do what God has called you to do?

You are loved. Whether you identify as male or as female. Whether you are OtherWise-gendered or struggling to find the words to explain your inmost being. You are loved.

Related Terms

Freedom - The ability to think or act independently, without hindrance or adverse consequences.

Liberation - Freedom from limitations that had been previously placed on thought or behavior.

Solidarity - Expressing tangible support for one another, around shared commitments or values.

YOUR NOTES

Afterword

Your Testimony

Very truly, I tell you,
we speak of what we know
and testify to what we have seen;
yet you do not receive our testimony.

John 3:11 NRSV

Context: Nicodemus comes to Jesus at night, and they discuss what it means to be "born again." This encounter includes the widely cited John 3:16 ("For God so loved the world ...").

No matter how much strength and confidence we may have, rejection is bound to sting a little (and sometimes it stings quite a lot). In John 3, Jesus is talking with Nicodemus, who was a member of the ruling council. Jesus chastises Nicodemus, noting that you (which is a plural "you" in the Greek) did not receive our testimony. To be more clear, let us say *"y'all* did not receive our testimony."

I find this such an interesting accusation. Nicodemus begins by praising Jesus, so this was not so much a personal grudge between these two men. Nor does it seem like a rebuke because Nicodemus was failing to follow Jesus. Somehow, these were two representatives of two different groups or camps who had not been getting along.

Jesus was pointing out that #TeamNicodemus had been discounting the testimonies of the Jesus people. I have to wonder what the disconnect was really about. Nicodemus and Jesus were both religious leaders, so I think we can assume that this was not a divide between religious and non-religious people.

Jesus says, "we speak of what we know and testify to what we have seen." So, the testimonies being rejected by #TeamNicodemus do not seem to be technical disagreements about the law. The Jesus people are speaking from their own lived experience. For some reason, #TeamNicodemus thought they knew better.

OtherWise-gendered people get this a lot. People with books and degrees and credentials like to explain about where and how we are supposed to fit into the big picture. Yet, they often do not take us seriously when we talk about our lived experience—or as Jesus put it, when we talk about what we know and what we have seen. When we speak about what we have been going through, it is not just religious people who filter our testimonies through their theories and arguments. It is also doctors and lawyers and social workers and all the rest, on down to family members and significant others.

It is no wonder that so many of us have faced rejection and even censure from religious authorities. The world has taught us that our experience is not to be trusted. Yet, we would do well to remember that even the people who knew Jesus face-to-face were being discounted—and that Jesus responded to the disrespect that they were shown by arguing that their testimonies ought to be heard. Jesus wants all of our testimonies to be taken seriously.

Have you ever been on #TeamNicodemus, discounting someone else's testimony? Are there people in your life whose testimonies you have found hard to believe? What parts of your lived experience do you hesitate to reveal to others, for fear of rejection? What stories of transformation do you have yet to share?

Praise God! Jesus invites Nicodemus—and each one of us—to begin again. May we be courageous when we face those who do not believe us.

You are loved. When you know what you know. When you struggle with rejection. When you listen to the testimonies of those who have been through it. You are loved.

YOUR NOTES

Appendix

Psalms for the Journey

I AM

I am who I am.

I am made in the image of God. The God of oceans and mountains. Maker of caterpillars and orchids. You are also the Creator of me.

I am who I am.

I am known, inside and out, by this God of history and mystery. By One who sees through my masks and pretenses. You even hold me in all of my fears and anxieties. My God.

I am who I am.

God saw me and declared that I am good. In all of my idiosyncrasies, I am good. In all my imperfections, I am loved. I am a blessed reflection of your majesty, O my God.

I am who I am.

I am full of gratitude and unexpected delight as you, God, reveal yourself to me, day by day. Even me, O God. Even me. May I find yet more of your light within me.

I am who I am.

See also: Genesis 1, Psalm 139.

Between

God spoke Logos and Sophia, Word and Wisdom. We are between. Male and female.

We are in your midst.

The Great Maker of mysteries divided the dry land from the oceans. We live at the shoreline of creation, where waves crash and sand moves. We are both. We are neither.

We are alive with possibility.

In those first days, there was day and night. We rose at your dawning and we will remain as your people at twilight. We will carry light into the darkness, just as stars shine in the night sky to remind us of your glory. With each new day, we bring hope for a better tomorrow.

We are the sacred in-between.

God made birds that fly and fish that swim. Has not God also made the platypus—a mammal with a mouth like a duck and eyes like a fish who walks like a reptile? We who may be unexpected. We who may even be called a hoax, or someone's cruel joke. All of us belong to you!

We bear witness to many ways of being whole.

We live at the crossroads, dodging traffic, somewhere between yesterday and tomorrow. We were made by the Holy One, the God of all that is.

Call us what you will. I am. We are. Neither. Both. Beloved. Good.

See also: Genesis 1, Proverbs 4, John 1, as well as "Zone of Rarity" by J Mase III in *And Then I Got Fired: One Transqueer's Reflections on Grief, Unemployment & Inappropriate Jokes about Death* (2019), and "Twilight People" by Rabbi Reuben Zellman.

Wrestling Within Me

The path before me is uncertain.
How can I know the mind of God?
Which way should I go?

Like Abraham negotiating for Sodom,
I am pleading for my future and struggling with my past.
May God be merciful for there must be some goodness left for me.

Like Rebecca questioning the life struggling within her,
My body betrays me.
I do not know how I can go on, O Holy One.

Like Jacob wrestling with an angel,
I am wounded and worn.
How long must I fight?

Like Jonah running away from God's call,
I want to throw myself overboard and be done with it all.
My God, please catch me.
Set my feet upon the path which you have set for me.

When will this battle end?
Save me, O Lord, in your mercy.
Give me peace.

The path before me is uncertain.
How can I know the mind of God?
Which way should I go?

See also: Genesis 18, 25, 32; Jonah 1; Psalm 69.

Putting on the Princess Dress

I put my faith in God.
Pulling on the princess dress my father gave me.

I put my faith in God.
Dancing in the tents, for your name's sake.

I put my faith in God.
Dreaming in the night of a better day for my people.

I put my faith in God.
They have come for me. Rising up against me.

I put my faith in God.
Beaten and torn. Prisoner in another land. Surviving.

I put my faith in God.
I run from unrighteousness.

I put my faith in God.
I offer up my best wisdom.

I put my faith in God.
I am lifted up. I am restored.

I put my faith in God.
They have come for me.
Reunited.

I put my faith in God.
They have come for me.
They carry me home.

See also: Genesis 37–50.

Blessed Be

Loved ones,

Seek justice,
and love mercy,
and journey humbly
with your God.

You who were born into exile,
will return to your homeland
amidst great rejoicing.

You who have been harmed
will be made whole,
and your scars will be
a welcome offering unto God.

Blessed are you who
hold fast to justice,
and seek righteousness,
and turn from evil.

For I will gather you under my wing,
and you shall be comforted forever more.

See also: Micah 6:8, Isaiah 56, Matthew 19:12.

On This Wildernesses Road

I walk on this wilderness road.
On a crowded street. Alone.

I am abandoned, but I am free.
What shall become of me?

A stranger approaches
comes to my side,
inquiring with curiosity.

We speak of the ancestors
We talk about children.

I am filled with purpose,
renewed in the promise.

Nothing shall prevent me
from singing the praises
To the Holy One
who has brought me hope.

See also: Acts 8.

Freedom

My redeemer has come.

You have made a way
Where I saw none.

You have confronted my enemies
And made my path clear.

You have sent friends to
journey with me.

I will continually dance
In your presence.

No more will I fear
Those who stand against me

Even when the way seems narrow
For you have encouraged me.

I will rest in you.

See also: Psalm 23.

Acknowledgements

Thank you to Crystal Cheatham and Our Bible App for inspiring me to begin this project.

Thank you to Audre Lorde, Peterson Toscano, Joy Ladin, Rueben Zellman, Elliot Kukla, and Eric Thomas for the work cited in each chapter.

Thank you to Louis Mitchell for suggestions on my first draft. Thank you to Nancy Krody for expert copy-editing advice. Thank you to Ron and Carolyn Paige for never-ending, unconditional support, as well as for being early readers.

Additional Resources

from OtherWise Engaged Publishing

Most of the themes of this booklet (plus many more) are developed further in *OtherWise Christian: A Guidebook for Transgender Liberation* (2019) by Mx Chris Paige, which includes an extensive bibliography of additional resources.

There is also a free *OtherWise Christian* group discussion guide. Available wherever you buy books. Paperback books are available from the publisher at a 60% discount if you order 5 or more copies.

Watch for the forthcoming *OtherWise Christian 2: Stories of Resistance*, an anthology edited by Mx. Chris Paige. Available in 2020 wherever you buy books (or ebooks).

You can sign up for updates from OtherWise Engaged Publishing to hear about other new releases as they become available. Visit http://otherwiseengaged4u.wordpress.com.

About the Author

Mx Chris Paige

Mx Chris Paige is the author of *OtherWise Christian: A Guidebook for Transgender Liberation*, publisher of OtherWise Engaged Publishing, and blogs daily at otherwisechristian.com.

Mx Chris was founding executive director of Transfaith and publisher of *The Other Side* magazine. They are available for speaking, teaching, and preaching.

Praise for *OtherWise Christian*

"This is the book that we need."

The Rev. Terri Stewart
United Methodist Alliance for Transgender Inclusion (UMATI)

"The most exhaustive look at gender non-conforming/trans identities in the Bible that I have seen to date. Informative & accessible... If you like *Transfigurations*, you will LOVE *OtherWise Christian*! "

Peterson Toscano
Author, *Transfigurations: Transgressing Gender in the Bible*

"I am excited to revisit familiar characters and narratives with a new OtherWise lens. This is an extraordinary gift to the trans community and to those, whether transgender or cisgender, who wish to go deeper in the texts to see those of us who have been hidden, erased, and/or disparaged."

The Rev. Louis Mitchell
Executive Director of Transfaith

"Chris has written an effective guidebook for transgender people of faith because the style is both scholarly, accessible, and respectfully penetrating in its biblical interpretation...There is a lot to like in *OtherWise Christian*, like Chris's enthusiasm about the way biblical interpretation will be enriched as people learn to read through liberated lenses..."

Dr Virginia Mollenkott
Author, *Omnigender: A Trans-Religious Approach*, 12 other books, and numerous articles

"...a truly incredible book. Mx Chris' writing is clear, elegant, and prophetic, and the book's intertextual readings of scripture and popular culture are very insightful. This book beautifully answers the deepest possible question: how can we imagine and practice our spirituality in ways that are truly just and liberatory, especially as it concerns our gender."

Cleis Abeni/Upāsikā tree
Transgender elder

"...a wonderful resource... This is a faith text that CANNOT be ignored."

The Rev. Shanea D. Leonard
Associate for Gender & Racial Justice for the Presbyterian Church (U.S.A.)

"...a brilliant yet down-to-earth, supremely compassionate and practical guide for how religious people who don't fit binary categories can engage with and draw strength from the Bible... Though addressed to those who identify as Christian, this book... does a marvelous job of reaching out toward non-Christian religions, particularly Judaism. "

Dr Joy Ladin
Author, *The Soul of the Stranger: Reading God and Torah from a Transgender Perspective*

OtherWise Engaged Publishing

OtherWise Engaged Publishing is excited to be working with the best and brightest of OtherWise-gendered folk! We provide a multi-tradition, independent publishing operation for projects from OtherWise-gendered folk that are in alignment with our values.

Visit otherwiseengaged4u.wordpress.com
for information about our latest releases
and to support independent transgender-led publishing.

What are the words you do not yet have?
What do you need to say?
What are the tyrannies you swallow day by day
and attempt to make your own,
until you will sicken and die of them, still in silence.

~ Audre Lorde

Made in the USA
Lexington, KY
03 November 2019